For St[...]

   Again [...]
times over, thank you for
your support, guidance &
mentorship all these years.
I hope you enjoy the book!

                    -Ellie

The Dwell

The Dwell

POEMS BY ELEANOR JOHNSON

Scrambler Books – Davis, California
2009

The Dwell
First Printing – United States of America
©2009 Eleanor Johnson

Cover art by Gerry Mak

Published by Scrambler Books
www.thescrambler.com
Poetry Series – Book 3

ISBN: 978-0-578-02736-4

These poems are dedicated to my beloved sisters.

Table of Contents

The Solomon Psalm

Continue, era of decadent manuscripts.

The earth has become a disintegrate writtenness,

quiet, unable to move, quite unable to stand.

Continue, era of mystified cadences.

The song has become as a lull, or the dwell in a

pendulum's swing, at the low point, the still or the chime.

We converge: the keeping of times, the kept motions,

memories of hearing and reading as singing and saying.

We converge: the emergence of time as motion, the urgent

motions as movements, as sung things or singings.

We converge: the story collapsed, the house down,

fire as madness, as grasping or crashing.

We converge: and manuscripts burning at once

tinder and tender, oh, tender as lovers.

As lovers we say strange things

strangely in strange hours

as though they were familiar

hours and ways of saying

just things to someone known.

We say things are like things:

your name is like the temple.

Your name, a thing built

of slow, round, poured stone,

its pallor hard and haunting.

Your name is as ointment

culled from sweet leaves

and cooling in fading sunlight.

We say these things as things.

We say these things as lovers.

As we say, we are singing.

We sing, as we are aroused.

Ours is an ambient arousal,

among which grow burning cedars.

Among the burning, cedars grow

as a consideration of fire.

Consideration: the togetherness of stars.

Burning cedars grow, still burning.

The burning cedars grow burning

as a consideration of fire, then fall

in symphony with each other, with stars,

which are always falling, always on fire.

The house is on fire in its parts of cedar.

The house on fire is in parts of stars.

It sings as it collapses, o sympathy of stars.

We are aroused by the crashing of the house.

We are aroused by the symphony of stars.

We are aroused by the burning of cedars,

and by their blue and orange singing.

We are aroused by blue.

We are aroused by orange.

We are aroused, and we sing:

amid falling timbers, we sing, fragrant,

heavy and luminous timbers, we sing:

we are on fire in our parts of cedar,

we are on fire in our parts of stars:

our parts of cedar as parts of stars.

And as we burn, we sing:

Lily, my lily, my lily, my love.

My love still feeds among the lily,

at the bottom of the garden of cinnamon.

Lily, my lily, my lily, my love.

The lily is the linger of the covenant.

Lily, my lily, my lily, my love.

Let us say how beautiful our lily,

among the burning cedars.

Let us proclaim our lilies beauties

while making adjurations to others:

we adjure you, daughters of Bethlehem.

We adjure you, soldiers of Lebanon.

We adjure you, king of the temple mount.

We adjure you, builder of mountaintops.

We adjure you: witness their fallenness.

We adjure you, keeper of the vineyard of Engedi.

Yes, you in particular are adjured,

keeper of the vineyard of Engedi:

we adjure you, harvest no dessicate grapes.

We adjure you, harvest our seeds of our songs.

The voice of the turtle echoes,

softly ampling among the dawn.

The turtle sings: My soul is liquefied.

We adjure you, turtle: hold still.

We must learn to sing slow:

sound moves slower than before.

We embody the name of the monster.

We embody the name of the monster unshaped.

We embody the shape of the liquid of souls.

We am the twinned, we am the twinning:

There has been a movement

to the foot of the temple.

There has been a movement,

a liquefaction, a slowing of souls.

We must sing more slowly.

We must sing more slowly

and repeat ourselves again.

We must name the places where we sing.

Cedar and cypress and cypress and cedar:

Heshbon, Damascus, Bathrabbim, Lebanon.

Lebanon, Heshbon, Damascus, and Bathrabbim.

Heshbon means limit of incantation.

Bathrabbim means tear of the bond of bodies.

We sing a system of beautiful places.

We sing a system of the beautiful.

Beautiful places collect our hours

into sandgrains, into hardness,

into heard things, and sung.

When the beautiful places are collected

we examine them, awaiting the flames:

Oh the vehemence of flame.

Oh the vehemence of flame.

We ask what the vehement flames mean,

and in our asking, we refrain.

There is nothing that fire refrains from.

There is nothing that remains of the rainstorm:

we breath beneath the eighth color of the vow.

Utter Things

When a man says to a woman:

Comfort me with apples,

he surely means her to cut the apple into parts.

He surely means:

Comfort me with parts of apples.

He surely means:

Let me take this apple in parts.

What he means by apples is songs.

What he means by apples is sung things.

By parts of apples he means parts of songs.

By parts of apples he means echoes.

A man says:

Comfort me with echoes.

Comfort me with the utter part of singing.

A woman says:

As a bird is a flight,

An arrow-struck bird,

its sudden wings folded flat,

is an echo of a bird,

a black breached belly

scarlet, belies the ease of flight,

down falls down like vows

sown in high winds or light

trapped in thick ground fog,

ground fog a suspension of rain

in stunned air, neither water nor wind.

I cannot comfort you with echoes.

I am not a sung thing or a thing of singing.

I am a suspension of parts, a ground fog.

A woman says:

Echoes are the keep of wraiths.

I promise you new made things,

from what was tendrillaneous and fine,

a diaphanous snarling of things woven,

a gossamer shimmer of ghosts.

I promise not a part of things,

but a thing apart from things.

Ghosts do not participate in things,

but make echoes.

A man says:

I do not want ghosts, but parts of apples.

I do not want woven things, but echoes.

I do not want you to make things, but speak back.

I am a hewn place of stone

as a soft place of camphor:

I am chanting chambers, echoing

heard things, beating phantom

landscapes into crumbling walls,

calling culverts and fjorded places

to purl into skeinish muscle

of dry, white shoreline, my dry, white body.

No steady sound along the shores,

along my body, there is only hewn stone,

echoing: I am a mapping of hours.

a mapping of forgotten things,

and I do not know your face

from thy eyes, thy hands, your taste

for suffering, where you are

and why so enclosed from me.

The woman says:

In this your difficulty of enclosure

is a difficulty of parts.

Parts of things are enclosed

from things and from other parts

of the thing; in this, the essence of parts,

and partings.

The man says:

I am a part of this thing and enclosed from you.

The woman says:

In this, we are both parts of things, and alike.

The least part of the lyre is the lyre string.

The lyre string is enclosed from the lyre,

the lyre from the baseboard from the bow.

A man says:

Long ago, you uttered in my ear,

"When I was a child, I could not recognize the moon.

I called it 'moon,' but meant the white, jade plate."

I was a long time under this uttered thing.

Words, the flat place,

cannot hold one such as you.

Teach me the old round songs

of old round gods.

The woman says:

I will purge the sky by parts:

of the shapes of the full enough spaces

of the lines of motion

of the motion of the stars

of the stars of the spool of heaven,

of the heaven of gathered things,

of the things of the breathing of the gods of words

of the words of the gods of breath

of the breath of worlds.

Of the heaving of the stars

of the heaving of the spheres

of the heaving of the shapes of spheres

of the spaces of the shapes.

Of the lines of the fullness of verse.

Of the verse of the lines of the shapes of spheres,

of the regions of the circles of the earth

of the circles the earth of sky

of the clouds of matter

of the matter of verse

of the verse of wood.

Now the gods' round songs

are shapeless, wanting sculpting.

The man says:

The moon settles low in the South.

I am singing a song in your mouth,

peony-shaped, the song, my mouth

at once open, catching air and light,

and tightly bound, dripping nectar.

The moon, low, in the South

catches us in a loft of light;

we laugh, lift our limbs and

shake them, and silent our way

into the almond orchard,

among the still glisten

of the moon, low, in the South,

you say let us taste almonds

on our tongue, hold their lines

parallel to our teeth, their flatness

vertical, bite down on fault lines,

to make the smooth surface come,

where our tongue can play

as lambent candle light.

The moon hangs low in the south,

seeking passage through a window

and into an old love's glazy eye,

or your lilting fingers on my cheek,

back, stomach, hip cradle, ankle

gentle into the crave of my bones.

The woman says:

Talking has become a weariness.

The man says:

Talking has become a manifestation of weariness.

Weariness has become a referent of talking.

Weary has become a loud word.

Talking has become writing.

Talking has become written things.

Writing has become a weariness.

Writing has become a weariness of referent.

Writing has become a talking with weariness.

Weary has become my bones.

Weary has become my ears.

My ears has become of still bones.

A fatal tonic has passed through the jamb.

It has passed under the door and into my house.

It has passed into my house as thy house

It has passed into my house as a scent.

It has passed as a scent into my wheaten bread.

It has passed as my wheaten bread into my daughters.

It has passed into the beautiful things of my home.

The woman says:

Mountains and rivers display their support of the painted doors.

The painted doors surround the made fortifications.

The mountains and rivers display the paintedness of the doors.

As such, they affirm paintedness, and the pavilion.

Unpainted doors may be torn down, or off.

Painted things can unpaint, become unpainted things.

In unpaintedness, they dwell briefly as unpainted

before they become just things, sitting around spaces

reminding no one of shapes or sung things that filled

the spaces that had been called buildings.

Thus, go the unpainted doors and with them built things.

The unpainted doors are not long as unpainted doors.

They are unpainted things, things sitting around space.

The mountains and rivers know this,

and thus reserve their display for painted doors.

The man says:

You have done me harm.

The woman says:

I have done you harmony.

How still the air where your face, my love,

the still air so still it will not still itself

my love, how still you are, my thing,

my own, my owned, my air, my other thing,

how still the air where once were stillings.

And my ears your hollow gourds for whistles.

Your still lips are kissed to purple still,

again, so many bruises, parts of purple,

making apples whole, how still thy lips:

the seventh color of the vow.

How stillness longs to be the heat-warped lyre

of some hard song, some beautiful song, and vile.

Oh, list: there's some singing again.

Oh, list: there's some uttered thing again.

The City Speaks

The sun breaks through me,

pink with veins,

a prism of water, held

by a skein of skin, barely

seeable except in faintest outline,

mapping our city:

my veins red roads,

my eyes littered lakes,

the birthmarks on my back

churches, skyscrapers, clinics,

homes, projects, terminals,

cathedrals, grocery stores, schools.

The space between them earth.

You wonder: how do I make love

to her.

When you embrace me

we defend poetry

as the secret structure of the city.

In our city

We are too quick to build type from instance,

pattern from particular, form from formed.

We need a course of antiaphoristics.

We need a course against generalizations.

We need a course of prosopagnosia,

The metonymic bias of reading faces

as a series of particulars that will not scan.

We need to say, eye, rather than,

proper name, common name, common man.

We need to see lips as lips, not signatures

of intention organized to speak.

We need this not just in reading faces, but all things.

We need a course of Sappho,

whose entire poetic corpus lies

in pieces, the more beautiful for

brokenness: ah excellent fragmentation.

Sappho's Treatise on Poetics reads, as written along a subway train

only
then
must
never
be
justified

Sappho's treatise on love reads, intoxicant menace:

You are the bright dancer,

I am the thick structure that holds you tightly moving.

Sappho's treatise on religion reads:

This is always the hour of conversion.

Conversion is not temporal,

thus does not happen.

Conversion does not occur.

Conversion is a settle of space.

Going to the city happens.

Going to the city occurs.

The city does not happen.

You know this already,

that you will go to the city.

Does your name not mean,

"Goes to the city?"

Does your name not mean in another language,

"Goes to the city?"

Does your name written in numerals not mean,

"Goes to the city?"

Your names occur as going to the city.

You must go to the city alone and

with the multitudes, with the dogs,

with the bicycles, the raw film.

You will all go to the city in ruins.

The city is the enfolding of space in stones.

The city is the convergence of stones in configurations.

And structures in a suspended state of collapse.

The city is the happenstance of conversion.

In the city, you will encounter madness,

the madness of stillness out of time.

In the city you will find conversion.

Madmen make the most meaning

out of the least substance.

They are not afraid to use strange tools.

They are very skilled at prophecy

who do not smile, but dance absently.

Perdues dans le non-sense d'un fou.

The mad men greet you familiarly

They greet you in an old language:

Elle est non or, elle est une noire,

mais voir n'est pas d'oir.

You will encounter mad Chiron

the centaur physician whose foot

is swollen with poison of the city:

Chiron, the mad doctor will warn you:

"Caution half-horse, half-men:

there has been a parting of blood.

Caution half-horse, half-men:

Your blood is in the city now

as rivers and roadways

that threaten no longer to lead

toward the bay, the highway.

Telegraph the gods:

blood has become directionless.

Caution half-horse, half men.

I'll soon be gone quite mad,

stamping my hoof maniacally

on wood foundations.

I'll say, ηψλε, ηψλε.

and make splinters.

Telegraph the gods:

Partings are in your blood too:

Stamp and say ηψλε, ηψλε.

Τελεγραπη τηε γοδσ."

You will say, oh caution.

It cannot be said that way.

Oh, caution, Chiron.

It would lead to ruins.

Oh, caution, caution.

It would lead to a new city.

And our gods are old and tired.

But as you say, you will be singing.

In the new city I sit under glass outside among others

likewise. Above us walks a pigeon. Above the pigeon

walks the sun, whose light illumines the pigeon's feet,

which I see from underneath, under glass. They are pink

with red veins. Another map of the city. And suddenly

I feel something: the heaving tenderness of seeing another

being transparent. Meanwhile, around me, the city drapes

its ruined body with echoes heard as prophecy.

The city will charge and beseech you

to read it, speak it, to write it, and hear it, all over.

For, there may be some matter,

in the center or at the periphery,

which is hanging unbuilt and waiting.

There may be a surplus of broken bricks,

Shattered glass, exposed foundations

Aut autem, aut autem, tam tamen, tam tam.

Dum stat neque, deinde stat nec

Dum stat neque, deinde stat nec.

Now is not the hour of questions,

but the midden-yard of rebuilding.

I am the half-mad centaur, I am the chorus.

You are the walker among hewn stones.

You are the wingspan of the city.

You are the emergency of thunderheads.

You are the drumming of the drum.

You are the drumming, drum the drum:

Aut autem, aut autem, tam tamen, tam tam.

Aut autem, aut autem, tam tamen, tam tam.

The List

I am secretly holding an ongoing magnetic event with LeCorbusier

concerning the ways meaning is created through built structures.

We am trying to remember the shape of a thing in general and particular.

We am remembering forgiveness by reinventing listing:

columns are lists of stones, pillars are lists of stones,

love is a list of stones.

I should mention that LeCorbusier is not

LeCorbusier's real name: random list of letters,

written sideways and spoken with a French accent.

Just as my real name is not Eleanor, but Eleonore.

Lists make one feel space as a series of particulars

through which the listing object slowly falls.

The the best lists do not list "in order."

They are accidental, a falling toward.

They are the testing ground of desire.

In this sense, the best list is the world.

There is a time for a love poem, but this is not that time.

Instead it is time for a new event: a poem about our city.

In our city, ugly lights fail as maps of intention,

on the ugly faces of ugly people on ugly mass transit,

transit filled with ugly carpet, ugly microbes, ugly air—

this is our city of ugly air, of ugly spaces.

We am committed to ugly.

LeCorbusier and I are ugly

mongers: behold this tangle of wretches!

behold the listing city, crumpled

and thrown down! People gather.

Our city is an association of possibilities and proximities,

close and in a state of falling, listing. (Bravo, bravo!)

Let it be shapeless and wild, an urban gangle of breaths.

Let it be listing and listless, for a little while.

 (Encore, encore, yes, that's it!)

There is the center of the city, there is the periphery.

(Bravo.) The round black parts represent round black parts.

(Bravo, bravo. Yes! LeCorbusier is the best.)

The steamship at the edge of the map

denotes a steamship, "a structure thrown upon the sea."

Let us throw upon the sea what is thrown upon the sea:

ships, fates, winds, flat stones, moonlight, wave-forms, bodies.

Let us throw our city upon the sea. Land is a dead medium.

We need to exploit other types of matter as sites for building.

Liquid, gas, plasma, and light.

(LeCorbusier is the best.)

The the lights dim, the curtain falls.

Through the darkness, we whisper.

A house is a machine for living in,

a stage is a machine for living on,

the sea is a machine for throwing on,

a steamship is a machine for throwing.

A poem is a machine for thinking in.

A house is a machine for living in,

A steamboat is a machine for transportation.

and a thing thrown upon the sea.

A poem is a machine for thinking with.

A list is a machine for making a poem:

we must learn to see airplanes

not as birds but as machines for flying:

we must abandon metaphor in mass transit,

we must abandon metaphor in buildings.

We must abandon metaphor in most areas

designated "public," such as bathrooms,

airplanes, steamships, the radio, television,

the internet, history, the Bible.

We must abandon metaphor in poetry as well:

a poem is a thinking machine

a poem is a thinking machine.

LeCorbusier and I are prisoners

of Berthold Brecht, like Julian of Norwich:

Over her head a cross, a bare bulb,

marked "cross," marked "bulb,"

the sound of labored breathing,

All shall be well, all may be well,

all can be well, all will be well...

The sign above our head tells you, "laugh."

And you are laughing.

1st Sonata: For Gaston Bachelard

The house I was not born in,

a Cape house on Cape Cod,

in Welfleet. I walk up across a path

of crushed bivalve shells,

Then five octagonal brick stones,

up one stair. The wind chime sounds,

but there is no wind.

The screen door is unlatched,

and I pull it open, the pump hisses.

The door handle is an old one,

Flat thumb place you press down,

Hook you pull on, brass, heavy.

Click the latch, push, the door opens,

a pleasing weight, more than most doors,

a step up, Persian carpet, laquered floor,

a brushed by a plant on the left side.

The lights are off in the house.

As I do not remember

where the switches are,

walking forward, my arms extended,

hands open, palms down, feeling air

buoying me up and forward,

a parent's hands under a first-step child's.

Sudden scent of bay leaves, a shaft of light

hits a woven green tapestry from Thailand:

I know where I am, the room is mapped.

In better light, I could see the yellow chair,

the sailboat painting over the hearth,

the grand piano and its woolen shawl.

In the corner of the room the chessboard

that broke my prideful boasting,

the marble table that broke my shins,

the windows that face the garden

in which I seduced a man many years ago,

ten years after my great-grandmother died,

the prickles of the squash vine against my knee,

were astonishingly sharp, the smell of the turned earth

strong so close to the ground, below the fence-line.

The room inhales; it can feel

my memories. I pass the card table,

drag my fingers across it, I feel the chip I worked

with my thumbnail. Ahead the toy chest

is open, I run my hands over familiar edges,

many soldiers, hard and painted smooth,

the dog doll I loved, its worn places, ribbon tongue.

It still wears my pink lanyard bracelet collar.

Though the jacks are spilled and dissipated.

A shaft of light, the mirror above the toy chest

Shows the entire room. I am not alone.

My great-grandmother stands by the settee.

She is wearing the bright orange polyester suit.

The white hair-piece bouffant on top.

Tan stockings. She looks like a cream-sicle.

The light is gone, she is still there.

Closer now, I hear her pills rattle

in her jacket pocket; her arm lifts.

I can feel her breathing around my face:

she has been eating beach plum jam.

Wrinkled fingers and long nails shaved

and sharpened to a point she used when painting,

trace my eyebrow, the bridge of my nose,

press my lips. I kiss back.

She pulls my head toward hers, we rest

our foreheads against each other, I know

our eyes are closed, because there are two

ways of being in the dark, separate and together.

My toes are curled around the edge of the carpet.

She lets me go, and I fall against the wooden wall.

She wears French perfume, and her trousers

Whisper differently as she passes by.

She will be going to the kitchen,

smooth blue formica countertops,

kitchen stools painted hot pink,

no one was thinking in the 1980s.

Refrigerator loaded with half-spoiled meats,

cookie jar pried, jam spoon in a coffee cup

in the deep porcelain sink, which drips:

Mnemosyne's metronome.

The screen door open, the flower vines,

Whose name I never knew, catching the wind

which has risen from nothing.

When she walks out that door, I know,

she will haul laundry off the line,

the round-headed clothespins will not splinter,

the cords will be dry, sheets stiff and cold.

2nd Sonata: Ekphrasis for Richard Serra

Penumbra walks with me among fifteen-foot twists of metal,

cochleal, dense, and rusting, or ovoid, dense, and rusting,

or concentric, dense and rusting, the post-industrial sublime.

Running inside them, I am the forgotten positron

in a condemned collider, in the middle of a dead city,

or a woman in an art installation in an opulent suburb

of Manhattan—it doesn't matter because the matter is so much

of what is already happening, it has become, as it were, obsolete.

Penumbra wins the race: light wings away, echoes unfurl,

sound trembles paralytic in the roundness that would be an apse

if this were a church, or cathedral, rather than a sculpted culvert.

Penumbra plays a victory song on his discordant factory pipes

and marionettes me. Dangle-limbs enjoined to dance the dance

of broken motions, wooden organs, painted blue tears,

evenly-spaced features I do not have. Head to the side, elbow high:

I always suspected there were strings from the ceiling;

there must be something about this wrought cavern

that makes them visible, their power feelable, there must be something about this wrought cavern that makes me

cavort my spastic tinder fingers into clattering hummingbirds,

my knick-knack arms into hingy serpents, my hips those

jointed and partitioned cloisonné fish you buy everywhere.

There must be something in the quality of gravity, light, mass

and my own speed as I turn inward more quickly:

my hands press the walls in the interior walkway

on either side of me, caught in the inner loop,

and I am a jealousy of minotaurs:

to be the lover of the structure that encases you,

roving its passages passionately, rapacious, wracked

with sweet confinement, every turn blocked,

beating horns against walls in furious ecstasy

at what is known too well.

How long have I been inside this vessel.

How long inside this city.

How long has Penumbra been laughing.

How long have I been singing.

3rd Sonata

I leave sleeping and barefoot,

the dim room sleep-breathing

curtains trembling eyelids:

it is a strange person, our bedroom,

like all persons, all bedrooms,

it only exists as such when occupied,

and I am strange to it, Grendel's

mother in Heorot: I want out.

The moments that define moments,

shifts between rooms or persons

of strange consciousness, states

of sleep and awakeness, I want

out: feet on the smooth wood, knotted

carpet, disorder of the senses

tighter, knotted carpet, woven rug,

smooth wood, my feet becoming

wiser, to the madeness of the floor,

growing vast claws that sink in

claws that sink in, and my hands

claw up: the doorknob a paradox

of impossible exits, torn from the frame,

the marsh-stalker hits the front porch

more a memory of a woman now

than a woman: echo of human form,

a curled shadow cast over a stone.

The fen-keen weird hag wants something,

does she, does she, she does, she does.

Wants to taste something. Talon-feet

slander the cohesion of pavement,

hands mock the cohesion of air,

body a nightmare of aesthetics,

cloaked by the darkness of pre-dawn

she hasps out laughter as an expurgation

of what was human once, but is now

an assemblage of rope, threaded through

striated fabric, smooth felt, wrapped over

rebar, rusted iron scraps, nails, and glass:

hasp, the gables gape, the glass glints,

projecting vision outward, beams of light

darkly, making darker what was dark,

a light most unfair, yes, she knows what

she wants now: corroded helmets, worn

suits of amour, scuffed and bloodied sheaths,

wreckage and battle-leavings, wreckage

from vines she has squeezed to death.

The motorcycle high beams catch her,

horrible screeching, a series of impacts:

a corroded helmet, worn suit of amour,

punched leather, scuffed, a foamy necked

prow, prey on her shoulder,

breathing slowly, slowly.

A bone scaffold pulled from wreckage,

sits on a plastic swingset, barely bleeding

beside an agglomeration he sees,

organized into the shape of a woman,

he wears tattered motorcycle gear, dented

helmet. Her ropes tense, taut

fabric over them, taming the rebar

of her warping, ghoulish skeleton.

He begins to scream, she is not a

woman, she is a demon, he cannot

even see her clearly, she is a demon,

built detritus of the city, assembled

from ravaged buildings, blown windows,

exposed girders, cross section of a subway

car, train, tunnel, interchange, track, station.

He is still screaming, what is wrong

with this city, what are you.

The moving system of ropes and rebar

reaches toward him, a furious smoothness

of motion: like the sea at the flotsam bourne,

like rural skies flocked with hailstones,

furious smoothness of falling motion.

As she almost touches him, her hand peels

apart: it is not nails, but textile, rent,

and rebar and corrugated iron siding,

melting before his eyes. Furious,

it dissolves, uncontact; beneath her arm

a pile of broken city accumulates,

arm melting, glass eyes dewy,

reflecting nothing. Everything shifts,

a new moment. He reaches toward her,

toothing his gloves off, racing off his helmet,

she is falling so slowly, he can see her now,

that she is naked, barefoot.

Holding her crumbling body

over the growing pile of rubble,

as though she will take shape again.

As though she will take shape.

But take shape from what?

The city, so eloquent in its decrepitude

shows little mercy for the discohering.

He rocks her like I cannot say.

Hasping and falling into a pile of

unquickness, slowly falling matter becomes

slowly nothing like fury. Stay with me.

On the plastic swingset, two separatenesses

take shape as one shape, shedding armor,

melting iron, fraying fabric,

discarded helmet, dented,

everything is shifted, she says,

this is the other side of the mere,

he says, shh, my name is Asher.

His arm holding what has emerged

from breaking and falling:

a small woman, of small furies,

who does not blink and does not smile,

but moves slowly, her back dancing chaos

on the bed of rebar she shed:

I am the moor bawn fen stepper

This is the other side of the mere:

We are beneath the city by a hundred

thousand years, we are beneath the city,

I am the violence that makes you

I am the keening, the horned gable

on fire, the torn thatching, the timber.

Shh, shh, they will come looking,

But they will not find you:

I am the fury Tisiphone:

I create the suffering of all

And my own: it is mine to mourn

All things sorrowful.

I am the suffering: I suffer holding,

I suffer building, I suffer structures

Imposed across my body, through it,

I suffer veins and muscles, bones,

I suffer order, planning, I suffer you.

Shh, will they come looking for us.

They will come. I will suffer them.

I am Tisiphone: mine is suffering.

I am Tisiphone, the fury of the city,

but they remember me as the hag,

Grendel's mother.

Ballet Ekphrases

Mark Morris' Three Mozarts

There was something

in the ballet like Spanish moss:

I know you know—being from the South,

being from drinking Maker's, being from open vowels,

being from people, being from—

what I mean.

I have been unable to put the dance from my mind,

a thin flame running under my

distraction, which, as you know, my friend,

has been mighty lately, lifting like a bird

from a high wire by a surge: thin fire, a crisp

of wings, then nothing til it lands again:

Second movement, Mozart Piano Concerto.

I don't remember which one, my memory.

Ballet asks a particular ekphrasis. Ballet is a virus, dead unless hosted. The

stage is its vector, a concession to vulnerability. Staged art is vulnerable,

ceases to exist if you leave, has never existed if you have not seen.

Second movement, Mozart Piano Concerto

and they were all of motion, we of voyeur. They faced each other, a

wreath of muscle, arms clasped in a ring—I thought of the plague years—

their bodies excluded us—we were the unfavored children—they the

beautiful. She fell, and it was meant, they all fell slightly with her, and that

is all the difference: the falling an event, a flow of intent.

And we all felt proud. It would not have been beautiful had we not been

there to witness: we gave it our eyes, our breathe: we gave it our breath,

and our held breath buoyed the fallen up again, in an embrace of

forgiveness or eros, I forget which one, my memory, ah yes, in an embrace

of eris.

Dance dance that exists apart from the real world, and that makes dancing

in the real world real by existing apart from it. That is why God made time,

I think, and motion: stages for forgiveness or eros, I forget which one it

was, my memory. So there they were, six lank dancers, looped and

spooling out, circles of motion like the world. That is why God made time:

to put music into, and bodies. It was eris, yes.

The first body on the edge fell and I heard it speak,

mercy, the sigh of arms and the embrace:

a body in the center, I thought of Kepler, my memory.

Second movement, Mozart Piano Concerto

kept beginning: a keep, and a beginning, a keep, and a beginning: a

beginning, kept.

The circle shed one dancer after another, a windmill shedding blades in a

light breeze, Mozart a light breeze, gentle, gentle. One must be gentle to

feel the technique as a rhyme, slant, feminine, falling, gentle, gentle.

I read about Pelagian fish—did I tell you this? (I know I didn't but like the

feint of redundancy, a comfortable moccasin, your favorite shoe)—

apparently, when large schools of fish turn, it's because one or a few fish

among them have become temporary leader-fish, who move their bodies

in the water a split second before all the other fish, and all the other fish

follow suit: a sheet of silver in the sea, turned sudden bright by the will of

one turning into sunfolds. Pelagius was a late Antique philosopher would

believed in the absolute power of human free will. Naturally Pelagius was

condemned as a heretic. Augustine was afraid of Pelagius, just as Mozart

was afraid of his father, Kepler of God: I come from you, you make me

make beautiful things.

You make me make things.

I am happy that you love ballet. I am happy that you are my friend. I am happy you write poetry. I look forward to your letter, very much.

I suppose I should end this letter now.

But first, remember how the dancers lay on their backs and put their arms up like calla lilies waving at the sky? It was a dance at death, they were on their backs, there was earth, their arms pierced up through the earth, their hands were calla lilies that waved and we were innocents playing checkers on a checkered blanket in our seats among lilies at Zellerbach? It was amazing, tonic as Madeleines, made me remember what has not been yet, reminded me of what good times it will have been, and how it will have been a picnic plunked on a field of calla lilies who stretch up things under the earth, I like how the dancers made death seem casual.

I should really end this letter now, my friend.

Love,

E

Alonzo King's Long Seventeenth Century

I am most aggrieved each time I think on your illness, its sombre

prohibitions. My poor friend, that white room with chairs on the walls,

your too-too vascular head, waiting, while I, my eyes blown roses by the

end of the Baroque piece, wept gratitude for musculature, ligaments,

bones, and sound.

The program said

"baroque" meant

"irregular pearl."

Indeed it did.

Small woman

strong and fast

and I mean

fast and in *black*

her arms

flashes and arcs

I have never seen

fast ballet

a treason against Ballanchine

there I was

not breathing

it was too fast

to time my air to.

The pas de deux, and here I'll stick to prose because the enjambements were enough already and more than enough: they were impossible. They were impossibility together. His body was so large and he was a black man, so beautiful; she, small, wiry; a baroque. They danced as though restraining each other, and it was his gift to seem restrainable, when really it is not possible to restrain what he was: so much beauty that it was enough, enough beauty, enoughness.

But he made it look *like* he was restrained: when I stopped my ears of harpsichord song, I could see straight enough and he was holding her above the ground, but when I let my ears gap up with tensile stings of plucked strings, I was confused by the enough and I believed she was restraining him. They were all folding together, one always stiff and strong and pliant and broken: iridescence born of rubbing.

The second half, tabla music, also baroque.

Three dancers, man, woman, the floor, a constantly shifting burial mound, their bodies thrown down and folded. It was impossible to tell who was

earth and who was body and who was digger and who was mourner.

They were an accident of dying motion, constantly but with decelerations.

Complicating matters, they were also making love.

Complicating complications, they were dressed in exercise trappings, black

leotards, white tights, pointe shoes. I am so in love with the picture I have

in my memory of their penultimate collapse. It was like this.

I hope your head will soon be entirely healed.

The ballet,

though enough

and impossible,

was not all it could have been,

in your absence.

In memory of the seventeenth century,

E

Mark Morris' Nutcracker

O give me my sin again.

I would like to have seen Shakespeare's own copy of *Romeo and Juliet*,

to see where he marked for actors to take breaths, or if.

Give me my sin

again: o

give me my sin again.

I would also like to have seen Mark Morris' own copy of *The Nutcracker*,

to see where he marked for dancers to take steps, or if.

I have just returned from his adaptation, *The Hard Nut*, and indeed, it was

just that—

a vast yonic flower dripping indecorous and fat from the ceiling,

a baffle of petal,

orchestrating ballet to the disencrypted

sexual tensions

and the mood I brought there,

small leather purse, leather flask shaped like a lipstick,

I was already there,

vascularized hibiscus dangled baldly before my eyes,

drastic cut-out nut hung high, both redundant.

I was a catastrophe/ of estrogens/ gone chestnut hunting// may the lord

our savior take pity/ and pour me another eggnog/ o give me my sin.

Notwithstanding what can only be called garish staging,

the dance was drinkable: merry as the season goes, the costuming

delightful, the foetid scent of egg-nog somewhere hovering in Zellerbach

amid children rubbing their eyes, blind to the fat yoni, fat nut, thank God

for that, and dear old Tchaikovsky.

A confession: I still find the sugar plum fairies intoxicating. A weakness for

what sparkles.

The Hard Nut plotline.

Resume: three young children forced to attend their parents' party,

glorious clothing, lavish gifts, slumber, rats descend, anthropomorphosis

(the Russian touch), seduction of a minor, then illness, storytelling (the

Russian touch), seduction of a minor, rats, arousal, realization that one's

child is in fact a woman. Some slumber (the Russian touch) that must have

been. I did not understand the relationship between the toymaker and

Marie, (the Russian touch) nor whether the Nutcracker eventually became

the toymaker's son, and human. I believe this represents a radical failure

on my part to suspend suspicion, and also to read liner notes.

Meanwhile, you're still recovering

from Bob Dylan

played by Cate Blanchett:

o era of improbable impersonations

that somehow work.

A puppet show for the discombobulated.

A metaphor for the jaded.

I would like to see a ballet for the disencrypted.

I tried to play an old Mendelssohn song on the piano while I was with the

man I should not have been with, and was surprised to note that all my

fingers held the song intact except the thumb on my left hand, which

dropped every other note. That must be something.   There must be

something to that.

I was in love with Drosselmeier for almost an hour.

There must be something to that.

The rats in this production were robotic

and controlled remotely:

a dark commentary

on ballet

tomorrow.

But, despite the shortage of funds to professional dance,

Mark Morris has a bathtub in his New York offices.

So would I,

had I offices

in New York or otherwhere,

a fleet of adoring athletes

pandering, but gracefully!

I think Mark Morris should make a ballet involving bathtubs, water dancing,

suds as tutus. I would like to see a wet and naked ballet in which none of

the dancers touched.

Hum. I have left the season, panting. It is time for a Pfeffernusse.

I do hope you will come caroling/ As with most things/ It will be more

pleasurable

In your company/ And I vow to you/ There will be no obligation/ To sing.

There must be something to that.

Let us promise to wear our Christmas best tomorrow at the party.

I will wear a green frock with red socks, a knit cap with small ears, and

mittens.

I imagine you will wear sunglasses, lovely drizzled earings, snakeskin boots,

and something orange.   I imagine you will laugh in the way you do.

When I was young, I played a game where I pretended I had dwindled to a

gnome and lived amidst the ornaments on our Christmas tree. I walked my

fingers along the branches, rows of cranberries and popcorn—mostly

popcorn—from small paper house to silken rocking horse, from knit Noel to

glass mouse.

Most of them were my mother's; I wonder if she thinks about them now.

Let us diminish ourselves, in a lovely way, the way of small fingers, and do

the *Nutcracker Suite* among the fir. We will nibble candy canes and throw

cranberries onto the floor, strut in minute and pointed shoes, balance in

minute and pointed hats.

We will dance the Russian dance in the dead of night, waking everyone.

Much love to you, my friend.

E

Bio

Eleanor Johnson is a poet, scholar, translator, and teacher. She studies medieval poetics, ethics, and literary theories. She has taught literature and creative writing at the University of California, Berkeley, and is an Assistant Professor of English and Comparative Literature at Columbia University. She has published poetry in the online magazine *Shampoo* and has a forthcoming collaborative book entitled _Her Many Feathered Bones_, from Achiote Press.

www.scramblerbooks.com